WAKE UP & LIVE

Powerful Methods for Achieving Your Dreams, Overcoming Adversity and Finding Happiness

JERMAIN MILLER

CONTENTS

Foreword vii

Introduction xi

Chapter 1: The Courage to Live 1

Chapter 2: Remove Roadblocks and Embrace Your Dreams 11

Chapter 3: The Magic Power of Belief 22

Chapter 4: Don't Just Stand There, Take the Leap 32

Chapter 5: Release Your Doubts and Drop the Burdens 41

Chapter 6: The Challenge is Big, But the Dream
            Must be Bigger 52

Chapter 7: Your Future Begins with You 62

Chapter 8: Life is Not Over, Get Back in The Race 73

You've got to be hungry if you're going to live your dream. Anyone looking to unlock their greatness, discover their purpose, and live their fullest, Wake Up & Live is the blueprint to show you how.

Les Brown
World's #1 Motivational Speaker
Author of *You've Got To Be Hungry*

I believe one of the most transformative choices we can make is to invest in our personal growth and development. Wake Up & Live invites you to explore a series of concepts and questions that will provide a roadmap to help you Win and Live the life of your dreams.

Dr. Stacie NC Grant
Chief Faithpreneur ®
Founder, Destiny Designers University ®

To Wake Up & Live is to know that one day, you will take your last breath. Before you do, to live means you have milked every ounce of sweat, blood, and tears out of the body that God gave you. EVERY DAY, ALL DAY, down to that second! This is what makes this book such a mandatory read; it inspires the reader to live their fullness every second of the day.

Byron Nelson
The Carpenter

Wake Up & Live inspires anyone looking to find the courage and develop the faith that no matter what obstacles they face in life, they can truly live their dreams.

Jamila T. Davis
Activist, TV Personality,
Best Selling Author of *Built to Outlast the Storm*

Jermain has written one of those timeless books that should be read over and over again.

Diana Nightingale
The First Lady Of Transformation

God hired us—a.k.a. gave us the gift of life. Our only job is to demonstrate our genius—a.k.a. unwrap our gift & share it with the world. Wake Up & Live gives you the principles.

Beyond Wynn
Investor, Coach Author of *Quotes and Confirmations*

"Every day you Wake Up, is a day
YOU can Live YOUR Dreams"

—Jermain Miller

FOREWORD

by Diana Nightingale

My first contact with Jermain Miller came about through a phone call regarding my late husband Earl Nightingale's messages. It quickly became apparent that Jermain and I were kindred souls, as evidenced by our three-hour conversation. That was several years ago, and we've shared many such conversations since that day, so when Jermain shared his new book with me and asked me to write the Foreword, I was more than happy to do so.

As I began to read his text, Jermain cut to the chase on the first page and eloquently described the global turmoil that we are all experiencing; but rather than rant on about all that is wrong in the world or placing blame—and he could have written two more books on that subject—he writes: "Now, more than ever, the world needs people with courage, those who can bring creativity and impact lives on the positive front. Leaders who can calm the rough waters and draw a blueprint for a greater future for all mankind."

I wanted to call him and tell him to go and look in a mirror, where he will see such a leader, because that's exactly what he does on all of the following pages—lead the reader to a calmer place and show them how to create their blueprint for a greater future for themselves and all mankind.

Each of us is a leader in one way or the other; we can lead others down a path to safe and happy places, or we can lead others down the path to destruction. One of the things we need to understand is that world leaders have a separate agenda other than to lead us down a path to safe and happy places. If that were not true, there would be no world wars, no discrimination of any kind. Instead, there would be justice for all. Each of us is a part of the whole; individually and together, we make things better, or collectively, we make things worse.

Jermain sums up the human condition and tells us exactly what each of us can do to pursue the lives that we imagine they can be, even in an otherwise seemingly uncaring world. He's found the source of all human suffering and its cure.

Jermain has the wisdom of a very old soul; he sees life as it truly is as opposed to how we may think it really is, and he also sees how to overcome the challenges we all must face in order to live meaningful lives. Jermain understands that whether it be the birth of an idea or the birth of a life, it takes time, expansion of self and a great deal of hard work and perseverance to fully appreciate life itself. Overcoming the challenges of life is how we finally come to know who we are, and can finally become the unique individuals we are all intended to be.

This is a book that should be read over and over and over again.

INTRODUCTION

George Bernard Shaw once said, "We don't stop playing because we grow old, we grow old because we stop playing."

I want you to think about where you are in life right now. Are you accomplishing the life of your dreams? Too often, we believe we have to wait until some magic hour to live our dreams—when everything is in order, but living like that has caused many to remain mentally paralyzed. Many people die, taking their hope of the future and all of their aspirations with them. They were living to exist and letting life take the living out of them.

If today was the last day you had to live and you knew it, what would you accomplish without fear? What would be some of the things, places and people you would try to see? What would you finally do? Sometimes in life, we need to take a step back and realize that despite how chaotic or challenging life can seem, we have a purpose. But this purpose will never be discovered by someone else; it can only be discovered as we dig within.

If you have not achieved your dreams and goals up to this point, what is something that will enable you to finally act? What are you looking to happen before you finally decide to live? The people who achieve their dreams in life look at the circumstances they are faced with, and if they don't like them, they don't become victims of them. Instead, they create the circumstances that they want. They believe in their dreams. Our belief system manifests what we believe is possible, and if we don't believe that we can have, be and do everything we've ever desired, we will never get there.

As you read Wake Up & Live, think about the things you want. What will give your life meaning and power? Start to believe that you are valuable. The life you want to live is worth living, but you must take action to reach it. When you take action towards something, you have hope for the future. And that hope gives you power in the present to carry you toward your destination.

But it is going to take courage and will to achieve the life of your dreams. Stand up to the small voice that says, "I can't" and believe that you can. Don't take these seconds lightly, but instead, take responsibility and ownership and make your life happen. Yes, life is hard, but these are the times that we must learn to get *from* life, not just through life.

Don't wait until it's too late. Wake up today and live the life of your dreams. There is a song you are supposed to sing, a book you're supposed to write, a business to be formed, a degree obtained, a home purchased for your family and people you must impact that only you can. Whatever dream it is that God gave you, only you can bring it to pass. Wherever you are in life now, no matter how difficult the road may seem, no matter how far away the dream may feel, your dreams are worth it. You are worth it. Your dream is calling you; the life you truly want to live is calling, and you can have it.

CHAPTER 1

The Courage to Live

He who has a why to live can
bear almost any how.
—Friedrich Nietzsche

As I'm writing this book, the world is currently facing two of the largest pandemics ever. The first one is the Coronavirus (COVID-19). The second pandemic is the fight for social justice against racism.

As the virus rages over borders and spreads across the earth, the world is also in an uproar over the wrongful death of another African American male by law enforcement, sparking a cry for change. There is currently no cure for the COVID-19 virus, and it has crippled the world and brought the economy to its knees. We do have a cure for the other virus we face, however, and that is REFORM. This call for reform has come in the form of protests, fights and even riots. Every hour that passes, people are glued to their TVs, social media, and news outlets.

In most parts of the world, there are curfews, stores are closed, and the economy has stalled as we try our best to get a handle on both of these deadly viruses. People are shut in at home and anxious, trying to figure out what this new "normal" will look like for them and their families.

Unfortunately, each day ends without any clarity as to where we will be tomorrow, and for many, this uncertainty breeds more fear. No one is exempt from the mental or physical effects of this pandemic. It doesn't matter how educated you are, how much money you have, or where your family is from—everyone is affected by the virus to some degree. Rollo May, in his great book, *A Man's Search for Himself,* said, "The opposite of courage in our society is not cowardice, it's conformity." Conformity, in this case, would be conforming to the fear of the unknown, which is presently crippling the masses.

Now more than ever, the world needs people with courage, those who can bring creativity and impact lives on the positive front. Leaders who can calm the rough waters and draw a blueprint for a greater future for all mankind. This lack in leadership should be obvious based on the rallies and protests that have recently taken place around the world as a cry against racism, despite the protestors knowing COVID-19 may place their lives in grave danger.

At present, many of us are surging with anxiety and doubt. What will impact people to *Wake Up and Live,* despite the current appearance of things?

Glued to the TV one day, I simply got tired of all the negativity going on. I would get so ashamed and angry just watching it all, and I decided I'd had enough. Right before I was about to turn the TV off, though—in the midst of the chaos, riots, fires, protests, teargas, gun violence and everything else that was going on—the cameraman picked up something that would change my life forever. I saw a person lying on a bench with covers pulled over their head.

It was at that moment that I asked myself a tough question: Where am I mentally, spiritually and physically throughout all of this? Am I lying somewhere with the covers pulled over my eyes, ignoring the events of the world as if I don't see anything, when actually I can do something about it? I thought about life, and how many people live their lives like that. Every day, they have an opportunity to live their dreams. But fear keeps them on mental benches, not moving and with covers pulled over their eyes.

After seeing the state of the world today, I was compelled to write this book because many of us (including myself) have been held back by a virus, one that attacks our thoughts and ideas for success. Over time, we have become victims of our own negative mindset, not even realizing we've set these traps ourselves.

One of the toughest challenges of living is knowing how to overcome adversity. When life knocks us down, when there are more losses and very few wins, when there are greater twists and turns and the world seems to be collapsing on us, what

3

exactly can we do? Many of us desperately want to Wake Up and Live the life of our dreams, but we are just too afraid to move forward. But even when there is uncertainty in our lives, we are still compelled to do something. Too often, however, that "something" is what we run away from. Only once we decide to dig deep within ourselves can we find the answers to life.

Socrates once said, "The unexamined life is not fit for human living." He meant there is a need for us to examine ourselves. If we are not consistently examining who we are and where we are going, then we aimlessly build a life that is not worth living. If we are honest with ourselves, we do want the life of our dreams to materialize. However, we allow our minds to stray and only focus on how to *not* have what we want. The worry about everything that could go wrong is where all the negative ideas are—the doubts, worries, and fears. For years we sit idle in such stresses, never taking any steps and never achieving our goals.

We must decide who we want to be, what we want to do, and what we want to have so we can align ourselves with our purpose.

Your Self-Assessment

Most of us suffer mentally because we think we can't do anything physically about our circumstances. Often, this thinking stems from the messes we made all those years ago,

4

the mistakes of the past. We dwell on what we did or didn't do, and hold ourselves hostage to regrets. But suffering, in and of itself, is meaningless. We give our suffering meaning in the way we respond to it. To live is to suffer, and to survive is to find meaning in suffering. Therefore, regardless of the circumstances, we can choose our attitude during times of adversity.

Please consider the following questions:

1. What is the meaning of suffering?
2. Can I live for something greater than me no matter how challenging or difficult life looks now?

Now, consider these answers:

1. Suffering: The state of undergoing pain, distress or hardship
2. Yes, you can live for something greater, but that something must be determined by what you want— not by what may be happening now. You must know where you are in life and that this moment is the sum of your every decision and action.

Things happen in our lives, and based on our level of awareness at that time, we respond. But our responses can evolve. Right now, I want you to list all the things that have been bothering you on a piece of paper. This is your "self-assessment." Write down all the things you feel you cannot get over, or the places where you feel mentally, physically, spiritually, and financially stuck. This assessment will help you determine your place on your life map and what is holding you back.

The first step in this process is to stop seeing the challenges of life, the things that bring pain, worry, and disappointment, as final conditions. The following are common hurdles many people face:

- ✓ Haven't completed school
- ✓ Dealing with bad health
- ✓ Spent time in prison (physical or mental)
- ✓ Had some traumatic experiences in youth
- ✓ Lost a job
- ✓ Failed marriage(s)
- ✓ Failed business(es)

Despite the hardships you have suffered, you can start over wherever you are now and produce a positive outcome. There may be some times in your past when you felt weak and gave in to things you now regret. But as you dwell on these mistakes and regrets—no matter how small—they will grow and fester in your mind. This deadly, virus-like thinking spreads and causes you to no longer believe in YOU!

Decide today that you have no time for anything that slows your progression. It's time to take the garbage out! Commit to no longer thinking about limitations in any form. If other people want to complain, don't allow them to dump their garbage on you. If the good old days are all you can think about, choose to think about today being a good day, as will all the days that follow. Get rid of everything around you that suggests anything other than the good you now desire.

Once we commit to change, we realize that what we have been doing is not an accurate reflection of who we are. It's a reflection of our inability to assess what has happened, so we don't go do the same things again. We have to dig deep and bring all our negative thoughts and actions to the surface to expose them. It may be disappointing, and it may be painful. It may take some time to expose them all, but until you do, life will not be able to progress to its fullest. When you are truly able to examine your life to remove all the negative things and see the good, then life becomes a life worth living.

At some point, we will all be forced to self-assess in order to move forward. Rather than wait for the perfect moment, when things seem calmer and easier, choose today to examine your thoughts and where you are headed because of them. Life won't allow you to keep putting off this self-assessment without consequence. If you are ever going to live the life of your dreams, no matter where you are in life, you must begin with a new mindset about who you are right now. This means changing perspective and looking at the same set of circumstances with different eyes—asking yourself, is there another way to view this?

It's reconsidering everything you believe about you.

We all hit rock bottom at some point in our lives. But the truth is, we don't have to "Do what we have to do" to survive. We can live our greatest life the moment we wake up and decide to do just that.

The Jumpstart to a New Future

What will inspire you during these challenging times is the will to live. You must embrace a quest for meaning and a desire to overcome difficulties. Many of us simply stay parked in convenient circumstances for years. They can also be the most uncomfortable circumstances, but because we are familiar with them, we would rather stay in our known hell than venture off into a strange heaven.

Here are three things you can do to give yourself a jumpstart towards your new future:

1. **Work.** What would you do right now if it were impossible for you to fail? Would it be something significant? Impactful? Most people don't do the things they love because they don't believe they can do them or don't know how to get paid to do them.

2. **Love.** When you look at your life, what are some things you love to do, even without pay? When we do the things we truly love, work feels effortless and time passes quickly. Think about why you're not doing

what you love, and how you can start to follow your passions.

3. **Courage.** What can you do today that you have been putting off because you didn't think yourself worthy? What have you delayed because fear has held you back? Decide today to advance with confidence in the direction of the new life you wish to live.

If you have been standing paralyzed on the sidelines of life, answering these questions will help you ignite the courage to step forward and live:

1. Think about where you are in life right now. Do you believe you have something more to live for?

   If yes, what is that one thing? If no, why do you feel that way?

2. With everything going on in the world today, do you find yourself mentally, physically and spiritually exhausted, with the covers pulled over your eyes?

   If yes, what is one thing you can do that will inspire you? If not, write one thing that you are doing to stay positive.

3. When unfortunate circumstances appear in your life, do you have the courage to push through them, or do you believe life is over?

4. The world needs leaders, people who are willing to do today what others won't do so they can have in the future what others won't have. Are you willing to be the leader?

5. Have you taken your self-assessment? If so, what are five things you are holding yourself hostage to that you need to release so you can live?

CHAPTER 2

Remove Roadblocks and Embrace Your Dreams

Either you act with authority in life, or
life will act with authority on you.
                                        —*Jermain Miller*

Where is the Will to Live?

What do you do when it seems like the world is on your shoulders? When everything you ever believed was possible for you no longer seems achievable? Do you sit back and let things happen, or do you get up and *make* the things you want to happen? If you have given up, I want to encourage you to demonstrate a new way of thinking. Our desires and goals are still achievable, but sometimes we give up without fighting hard and long enough, and reason ourselves out of believing in them.

Look back at all your childhood dreams. Remember how easily you could describe your future without limitations? There wasn't a care in the world and no such thing as reality. Throughout life, however, we face new challenges. We are met with what may seem like reality, and we become discouraged. However, we all experience the world through our own lenses and perspectives, and what we perceive as reality (and the possibilities that come with it) is not always true.

If we live long enough, there will be times when we may feel like a complete failure. But in reality, we were simply unaware of our true destiny during those times. We were striving for things and situations in life that did not belong to us. So failure, in this case, meant we did not measure up to the place we made in our own minds. This place represented a predicted station in life or a space we felt we should occupy at a certain time in our life.

Failing to meet these pre-set expectations is no indication of our potential and what we could accomplish, but what if it were? What if we truly did not measure up? What if we have lived our lives up to this point only operating on a tenth of what we could do—and so are not doing what we really desire to do? Deep down, we know we can become more, do more, and we should have more. Like a gentle touch, we feel it, but instead, we substitute convenience for the dream. This is not how we really want to live.

Johann Wolfgang von Goethe, the German philosopher, once said, "Before you can do something, you must be something." Life has a unique way of causing us to "be" before we can "do," and to have the life we want, we must "do" something.

We all have a turning point in our lives: this is the "Wake Up." That moment when we realize we have been living far below our fullest potential, and that yes, there is something better, something more, something greater for us. But how do we find the path to this destination, where all our efforts amount to winning and living well? If we intend to live this great life and be all we can possibly be, then why do we find ourselves still settling years later?

If we are honest with ourselves, most of us have simply lost our will to try. Living the best life now seems too vague and out of reach. Therefore, we find ourselves drowning in mediocrity. We live far beneath our capabilities, too timid to approach the potential within us.

Through the challenges of life, we become discouraged, frustrated, and feel let down. When things don't look the way we expect, our assumption is *This must be all there is to life. I'll fight my way through this, even though I don't have a plan to live beyond it. I can't see myself having, doing, and being any better than what I'm dealing with now.*

However, we can only receive what we see ourselves receiving.

I repeat: *"We can only receive what we see ourselves receiving."*

Knowing this, we must reevaluate our state of mind and our ability to live the life of our dreams. Far too often, we find ourselves placing too little value on our lives.

In order to live our best life, we must be acting under our own will—not the will of anyone else. Yes, we can be inspired or encouraged along the way by others, but we must take action to create the life we desire. The results we want only come when we do the work. Nevertheless, if we are going to accomplish the goals we set forth and live the life of our dreams, it is going to take the kind of strength and courage we aren't used to giving. It will *require* us to do things now that most people won't, so we can achieve the future that most won't have. But first, it starts with our willpower and deciding what we want.

Many of us believe that if we just exert our will, we can accomplish anything. Yet somehow, we do not exercise this line of thought. Therefore, we cannot reach the actual "willing" point. We put it off and talk vaguely of someday, though that day never comes. The desire for what we think we want simply isn't strong enough for our willpower to kick in.

If we really want the life of our dreams, we must develop the willpower to accomplish it.

Everyone has the potential to have a strong will. All we have to do is train our minds to make use of it. It is not our willpower that needs to be trained, but our mind.

American essayist Donald G. Mitchell once wrote, "Resolve is what makes a man manifest; not puny resolve, not crude determinations, not errant purpose—but that strong and indefatigable will which treads down difficulties and danger, as a boy treads down the heaving frost lands of winter; which kindles his eye and brain with a proud pulse beat toward the unattainable. Will makes men giants."

Stuck Outside Your Promised Land

The children of Israel were told they could have all the land they could see. In a way, this is also true for everyone—the amount of land we can have is contained in our mental vision, what we can see for ourselves. We can have anything we desire, but we must imagine it first. Every success, every goal achieved and every accomplishment has been brought into manifestation by holding onto a vision, even when the outside world doesn't mirror that image. Many times, right before the greatest turning point in our lives, we find ourselves stuck outside of our promised land and mired in setbacks, discouragement, and shame.

When the children of Israel reached the Promised Land, they were afraid to go in and take it. They said it was filled with giants who made them feel like grasshoppers.

> *And there we saw the giants . . . and we*
> *were in our own sight as grasshoppers.*
> Numbers 13:33 (KJV)

Many of us experience the same thing in our quest for the promised land—problems and tough times that also look like giants—things we fear. We never get to live our dream or reach our goals because we never go beyond our comfort zone. Thus, we are constantly stepping back into safety, stuck outside of our promised lands. This causes feelings of failure or the belief that life is somehow against us.

"Every time I turn around, something is going wrong," we complain. Yet we fail to realize the "wrong" is the set of circumstances that reveals who we truly are. The problem is that we convinced ourselves, much like the Israelites, that we are grasshoppers too. In doing so, we gave all our power to things we felt were stronger—the giants, the storms of life.

We can only be to others what we are first to ourselves. The key to building our dream life in dire circumstances is understanding our true possibilities. We must know our dreams. Going beyond what we see will require us to envision ourselves as giants and all adversity as nothing but grasshoppers. Trials (giants) only challenge us to become more and do more so that we can ultimately have more.

The Courage to Advance

Nothing stands in the way of someone who places their goals and dreams for their life above fear and worry. The fear of failure, sickness, and loss are worst-case scenarios we create for ourselves, and they are also the very reasons we are unable to move forward. Fear stands in the way of accomplishment.

According to Merriam-Webster, fear is "an unpleasant often strong emotion caused by anticipation or awareness of danger." It's worrying about all the things that may go wrong if we start a business, go back to school, try to save money, go on a diet, or leave a bad relationship. Having the will to live means leaving the known (what is familiar) and going toward the unknown (that which makes us uncomfortable).

Fear and having the will to live cannot coexist. Fear can cause a person to sit idle for years, leaving their dreams and the life they wanted far behind. They simply go through the motions of life with no ambition, no energy, no interest, and no will. The lack of drive becomes ingrained as they grow to believe that this moment they are in will remain the same for the rest of their lives. There is no point in trying for better.

Changing this kind of viewpoint takes courage, determination, and focus. To achieve your dreams, you must prepare mentally, even when your goals seem far away. You have to *do* something, and that something is having a desire and interest. The moment we really desire something, we become interested in achieving it. We focus and align with anything likely to help us accomplish it by creating new ideas in place of negative ones, ideas that turn the outcome in our favor.

Fear is not desire, and staying in a fear-based mindset won't allow you to obtain the good you desire. Until we understand that erroneous ideas cause negative results to manifest in our lives, we will not develop the courage it takes to change them. We will just keep heading in the wrong direction, hoping things get better. Henry David Thoreau once said, "If one advances confidently in the direction of his dreams, and endeavors to live the life which he has imagined, he will meet with a success unexpected in common hours."

When the Wright Brothers decided to fly, they didn't know how to invent the object that would take them into the sky—all they knew is that's what they wanted. During the course of their research, they experienced setback after setback. People thought they were crazy, yet they held on to their belief. Their own father, who was a religious leader, told them their ideas were no good and impossible, but they kept at it. They studied scientific theories, stayed up late, and spent all their time and money on their idea. The Wright Brothers kept trying and failing, but they held on to their vision. Then one day, it happened for them. That first flight lasted only twelve seconds, but this small victory would change the course of transportation throughout the world.

Meeting with success requires setting goals. It means waking up every day with the confidence and the belief that we can live our dreams. It's having the courage to move forward to a life worth living, even in the face of everything that may seem wrong. It's knowing that if we remain faithful to our vision, one day it will happen for us. And in the process, we will meet with success unexpected in common hours. Then our goals, dreams, and the courage to advance toward a life worth living will finally materialize.

People who have lived their greatest lives and risen to the highest heights in achievement usually experience an overwhelming amount of pushback before getting there. Just think of all the things a successful person goes through before they become a success. Typically, they have been misunderstood by friends and family; some may not have had even the bare necessities of life, but with belief and determination mixed with courage and the "will to live," they managed to hang on until their magic moment appeared.

William Hutchinson Murray once said, "Boldness has genius, power and magic in it." The genius is you, and the magic and power are what happens when you have the courage to live.

When we face the things we fear, fearlessly, they often fall away in that moment. Everyone will experience problems in life. What are yours? What is causing you to sit on the sidelines of life and not take any action? Yes, there may have been times in the past when you failed, but why did you fail? Did you fail because you didn't do anything, or did you quit before things turned around for you? How did you see yourself after this? Low, or no good, that you can't accomplish anything?

I want you to try again, but this time change the way you see yourself. Change the way you see the outcome in your life. Instead of thinking it will go wrong, think it will go right. This time, you will overcome every obstacle and challenge, every weakness, and achieve the victory over all your setbacks and circumstances.

How to See Yourself Better

A new ship was about to be launched in a coastal village. Constructed with great craftsmanship by the men who enjoyed their work, it was designed to sail the seas of the world, delivering and returning rich cargo. On the day of its departure, the town officials led the citizens on a happy march to the brand-new ship. The mayor gave a short speech, then raised his hand to signal the ship to slide into the sea. The crowd watched in expectation for the first sign of movement, but it never came. Once more, the mayor signaled for the launching, but again, nothing happened. When the workman investigated what could be stalling the ship, they discovered that some of the holding blocks had not been removed. As soon as those holding blocks were removed, the ship began its journey to its new destination.

Like the ship, we have to discover what's been holding us back from our dreams. I want you to close your eyes and see yourself strong, successful, happy, and full of life. See yourself walking a path that moves you toward your goals. Behind you, the air is gloomy, but if you keep your eyes on what's ahead, the path will start to brighten and fill with loveliness. See yourself climbing, winning, no longer being held back by old habits of falling and losing. See yourself meeting every difficulty with victory. See yourself sailing to your dreams.

How do you feel? Isn't it a great feeling to see yourself at your best self? This is what I want you to do every day. This is how you create the image of the life you want to live.

It is a well-known fact that the moment we begin thinking positively and moving toward our dreams, rising above what has kept us bound, everything seems to go wrong. Why is that? Well, once you start moving, things start shaking. Nothing stays the same when we move. In the past, we were stagnant; and when stagnant, everything remains in place.

Now, during this change, is when we must realize what our desires are and decide what we really want in life.

Below are a few points of reflection. Please answer according to the text you have read. Once you have answered, think about how you might apply some of the principles in this chapter to your life.

1. Define "will to live."

2. What is fear?

3. What is courage?

4. How do you set goals?

5. Have you ever failed at achieving a goal? How did you overcome it?

CHAPTER 3

The Magic Power of Belief

Circumstances only reveal who
we are to ourselves.

—Epictetus

What are You Doing About Your Future?

My mentor, Mr. Les Brown, once said, "The graveyard is the richest place on Earth, because it is here that you will find all the hopes and dreams that were never fulfilled, the books that were never written, the songs that were never sung, the inventions that were never shared, the cures that were never discovered, all because someone was too afraid to take that first step to carry out their dream."

In the depths of our souls, there is a driving belief that there is something more to life than the difficulty we may be facing. Our instincts tell us there is a better life for us, and that we can live the greatest life of our dreams. Somehow in the process of living, though, we convince ourselves there is no way out of where we currently are. So we become victims of defeat, living an unfulfilled life in quiet desperation. Many of us carry this mindset until our dying days, hoping for something new but never daring to try.

If we want to have, do, and be more, we need to decide what we want life to look like. Never should we be willing to accept less than the best when it comes to our health, happiness, peace, or prosperity. To have the very best, we must *define* what that means to us. Far too many people are depressed and beaten down by life because they just don't believe that life is worth living—that there's nothing more.

Often, we stay stuck in this thinking because we feel as if we deserve the beating life is giving us. Or maybe we feel that what we are going through is inevitable, simply a part of life. "It is something I must go through to get somewhere," we may say. But the question is, "Where?" Where exactly are we going while we're going through what we're going through today? We actually don't know. We don't know because there was never a clear, concrete destination, something we deliberately chose to be our end goal.

Every action, even a non-action, is a choice. So by doing nothing, we did make a choice—but we never chose the life we wanted to live. We end up somewhere we did not expect, an undefined location, and we accept the negatives and remain in bondage to it. So what are we going to do about our future? Are

23

we going to tolerate living less than the best? Or are we going to seize our own destiny and steer boldly toward our goals, regardless of what the present looks like now?

The exercises below act as a stepping stone to assist you in forming a plan for your future. Please be as detailed as possible.

1. Write down the life you really want, not the life you *think* you want. Be specific. For example: I am a proud owner of a successful business. I am happily married. I am finished with school. I am taking three vacations a year.

2. Write three negative conditions you want removed from your life. Once written down, decide how to take the steps to remove them—whether mentally or physically.

3. Organize a list of things you want to accomplish.

4. Take action toward the life you want to live. You can do that today by taking the following steps.

    •   Choose the easiest task first, then act on it immediately.

    •   Stop focusing on the things going wrong.

    •   Don't worry about what people may say.

    •   Surround yourself with positive images, people, books, ideas and goals.

You must decide the way you want to live. No longer should you be content with drifting along, hoping things will turn out better than they are. Overcome your own weaknesses and faults, no matter how often you may have failed in the past, or how horrible it may seem.

You can make the life you choose!

Just Because You did not Quit Does not Mean You Believed

Recently I found myself watching one of my all-time favorite movie series, *Rocky*. In the first movie, Rocky Balboa was an uneducated, kind-hearted, working-class Italian American boxer looking for a shot at his dream of being a champion. After months of hard work and training, he got a chance to fight the world champion, Apollo Creed. While Apollo Creed may have taken the fight to pad his win count, Rocky saw this as an opportunity to become someone he always wanted to be, and that was a winner.

All the things that Rocky had to overcome made me glad he got his shot at fighting the champion. Then, I watched Rocky in this championship opportunity get savagely beaten by Apollo Creed. The match was like nothing I had ever seen before. Round after round, I, just like most people who have watched the movie, sat there in agony, asking myself, "Why doesn't he just quit?"

In the fourteenth round, Apollo got the best of Rocky and knocked him down. This was probably more than the twentieth time. Thinking that he had landed the punch to finally take

Rocky out, Apollo went running to the corner, celebrating. In his head, this match was definitely over. He had given Rocky his all, and there was no coming back.

As the referee chanted the countdown, Rocky made his way to the ropes, pulled himself up, and got back on his feet. In complete shock, Apollo knew this was not his usual opponent. This was someone who wanted something, someone who had nothing to lose, someone who, no matter how many times he got knocked down, kept coming back again and again and again.

As I continued watching the fight, here's what I realized: Although Rocky was no quitter, he went on to lose the fight. That's because even though he hung in there, he never truly believed he could win.

So, as *Rocky 2* starts, we see Rocky and Apollo in the hospital. As Rocky is walking past Apollo's room, he stops and asks Apollo, "Did you give me your all?" Apollo looks at him and says, "Yes, I did give you my all."

At that moment, Rocky knows that if he were given another shot, he could beat Apollo. This time, it was not about hanging in there and losing. Instead, he felt a deep-seated belief that "This time I can win."

And, this time, Rocky wins the fight. Here is the difference between *Rocky* and *Rocky 2*. In *Rocky*, he wouldn't quit, but deep down, he did not believe he could win. In *Rocky 2*, he *believed deep down* he could win.

It may sometimes seem in life that every possible thing is going wrong. As you keep pushing through the struggle, ask yourself: Do I believe things will be better? Do I believe that there is more to life for me?

Though you may not have quit surviving, you also have not believed in the impossible for yourself. No, you may not have quit your family, or quit going to a place every day where you don't even want to be. That much is true, but the difference between achieving your greatness and simply surviving is in *your belief*.

So again I ask: Do you believe there is more for you? And if so, do you believe you have the capacity to attain it?

Napoleon Hill once said, "Whatever your mind can conceive and believe, it can achieve." That word conceive— there is the seed. The moment you think about your idea, that's *your* seed. Your job is to plant that seed by going to work on your ideas, goals, and dreams. If you don't have the seed, you cannot conceive. If you can't conceive, you will not believe. If you don't believe, you will not achieve.

You have to know that, no matter what is happening in your life, you believe you can succeed!

Traffic Control

Any aircraft flying to a destination is monitored by air traffic control. Their primary purpose is to make sure there are no collisions, provide information and other support for pilots, and direct the flow of air traffic.

We are all on our life journeys with the goal of getting to a destination—the life we want to live. Often, we find ourselves on an unknown journey because of fear or second-guessing our decision. We never had consistent, positive conversations about where we want to end up or who we want to be. Instead, we thought more about the possibility of things going wrong or something not turning out in our favor. If we do start positive conversations, the negative talk drowns the good out and causes mental collisions.

There is just too much traffic in our minds, and it can lead us to places we didn't want to go. That's why it is important to choose the destination and be certain it's where you want to end up—because there will be turbulence on the way. The only way for us to get there safely is by making sure our mind-traffic control is directing us correctly. This can be done through:

- words we say to ourselves
- affirmations we surround ourselves with
- prayer
- reading books
- our thoughts
- positive people we associate with
- belief in our goals

We are never given the vision for the journey. We are only given the vision for the dream. If we were given a sample of all the things we would have to go through—a step-by-step guide of all the hardships, pain, anxiety, sleepless nights, and heartbreak, then we would never get off the ground. We'd continue to talk ourselves right out of the dream.

But if we keep a clear vision of the dream, it will be our magnet to pull us through these tough times. When you see your dream and know it's yours, you act accordingly. You are confident, and it's the only thing you want—no matter what happens along the way.

There are a few steps you can take to stay focused on the dream.

Do not waste time worrying about adversity.

I recently went to a parent-teacher conference with my five-year-old son. I tried to sit down at the desk, and boy was it a struggle. These desks are not supposed to fit someone my age. Likewise, in life, here is where a lot of us get stuck. We waste time asking, "Why me?" Your dreams and goals are requiring you to grow, to advance to the next level. If you're no longer five years old, of course the desk should not fit you at twenty-five. If your dreams are big and your future is bright, the question you should ask yourself is, "Why not me? Why shouldn't I have to go through the adversity that makes me stronger? Why shouldn't I have to figure this out and grow so that I can impact others with my story of success?"

Don't let your doubts be louder than your dreams.

Shakespeare once said, "Our doubts are traitors and make us lose the good we oft might win by fearing to attempt." Too often, the fears we have of failure are based on self-imposed limitations or ideals. We destroy ourselves and beat ourselves up for not living up to an expectation. We are so concerned with what others might say to us or about us, we forget to pay attention to the things we say to ourselves. Find a group of people who will encourage, support, and push you along the way.

See setbacks as a chance to improve, not a path to failure.

When Rocky was preparing to fight Apollo, he trained day and night. And though he still lost, the things he learned during that training made him stronger for his next round. He was able to use his failure to build skills for success. Like Rocky, we may lose the first fight, but the skills we learn will stick with us, and we will be more prepared the next time.

Have you been stuck outside your promised land of dreams and goals? If so, the exercises below will unlock what has held you back.

1. We often talk about living our best lives, but that best life is undefined, so we never manifest it. List five things that, if accomplished, would be considered living a best life.

2. If you have been stuck in a mental slump for years believing life is not worth living, the truth is that what is worth living simply has not been discovered yet. I want you to think about one thing that would be impacted in a positive way by you changing your belief about you.

3. Have you found yourself still doing things you really don't want to do anymore because you feel you're no quitter, even if it is hurting you? If yes, name three things you would like freedom from.

4. Although you may feel like life is beating you down, it's not until you believe you can win do you win. Name something you were able to accomplish that you really wanted, despite the challenges at the time.

CHAPTER 4

Don't Just Stand There, Take the Leap

Do what is easy and life will be hard.
Do what is hard and life will be easy.
—*Les Brown*

The Revealing

One of the most significant ideas of the Stoics is that there are some things we have control over and some we do not. We spend most of our time trying to control life outside of us, instead of focusing on the things we can control. Our feelings about a situation may cause us to respond positively or negatively, but the only thing we can control is our actions.

Too often, we expect life to look one way, but our actions are taking us in a totally different direction. We may assume we are heading towards the life of our dreams, but that is based on our perception. To some, simply avoiding difficulties or finding the easiest path may be the goal. Opportunity, however, comes masked in the form of heartaches, setbacks, challenges, and adversity. When the odds are stacked so high against us and we just don't know what to do—it is at these points in our lives that the Greek philosophers' words become true. Circumstances don't make us; they only reveal who we are to ourselves. Although we can't choose our circumstances, we can choose what we think, and that indirectly shapes what we do in our lives.

If we find ourselves going to a job we don't like, or we're unfulfilled and unhappy in a relationship, this is not living the life we want. We must do something about it. Begging to have better but unwilling to do what's necessary to improve ourselves so that better does happen isn't the way to go. What we are doing may be living, but we are merely living to exist. What holds us back is not the circumstances themselves, but the image we have of ourselves in the midst of them. Often, we are so occupied with things that do not matter that we don't take time to look inside ourselves.

Sometimes, life demands us to reevaluate what matters most. Often, we come to forks in the road that are tests that we didn't realize we needed to pass. But instead of changing, we continue with a "Do just enough to get by" mentality. So we live life unchangeable with our family, money, health and spirituality until it ultimately results in a downfall.

We sit waiting for circumstances to disappear without us doing anything about it. Ask the future you how you would look at the challenges you're facing today. They probably would not faze the future version of you one bit.

What do We do Now?

In my early teens, I watched the girls play Double Dutch. Double Dutch is a jump rope game where two people stand on opposite sides and turn two ropes one over the other. The third person must time the turning ropes perfectly to get into the center and begin jumping to avoid getting hit by the rope.

While my focus was not so much on the game itself, but more about girl watching, there were times when I attempted to play—but I never quite made it. I would stand on the side and fake the act of jumping, but I never decided to actually join in. I saw how much fun the people had when they did jump in, and I wanted to enjoy that feeling. However, I was more afraid of getting hit by the rope and people laughing at me than taking the leap and enjoying the game also. So I never fully committed. I played it safe.

Back then, I sat on the sidewalk, watching others enjoy life. And as I grew older, I found myself committing this same act, but now I was sitting and watching in areas of my professional life. I watched people experience their breakthroughs and live their dreams while I attempted to tiptoe toward mine.

At some moment, we must decide what will be the "jumping in" point of our life. We may know what we want; we may even be practicing from the sidewalk, planning for the right moment. But too often, we sit on the sidelines, watching others enjoy life because we are too afraid to take the leap.

Life has a way of making us believe that if we get hit by the ropes of life, then there's no coming back. However, this is not the time for us to lose sight of the joy of living and faith in our future. We can't spend all our time focusing on the rope. If that is our mindset, the future, even with all its possibilities, will be doomed. It is during our darkest hour, when it looks as if there is no way out, that we must not allow ourselves to decline.

If you have not yet discovered the meaning for your life, or perhaps you've lost your will to live and feel there is nothing left to truly live for, know this: Each of us has the power to envision, create and enjoy a fulfilling life. Discovering what that is, however, is up to us. We have to believe in ourselves and our God-given abilities to accomplish our dreams and reach our ultimate destiny.

We do not need freedom from adversity, but the freedom to take a stand toward it. It is possible to stand firm in what we believe amid hardships or struggles. Today is the day we decide that, regardless of the current circumstances, we will live.

Turning Fear into Faith

After Thomas Edison failed for the 9,999th time at inventing the incandescent lightbulb, he had a choice to make: Continue or give up. Fortunately for the world, Edison was not dismayed. Instead, he said, "I have not failed. I've just found 10,000 ways that won't work." He knew that if he kept going, learning from the mistakes, eventually, he would succeed. He spent all his time and energy on his work. To him, nothing else mattered, and he was able to bring his invention to life.

Edison didn't take too long celebrating his amazing invention, though; he went right on to the next. All in all, Edison would file 1093 patents, including the phonograph, motion picture camera and the incandescent light bulb. He has been described as America's greatest inventor, a passion he carried throughout his entire life.

We must understand that life will only reward us for the things we work on and complete. We don't get rewarded for incomplete projects.

Aristotle once said, "Excellence is unto completion." Excellence lies in us completing our goals, but sometimes, we stop and go on to other things before the work is done. We continue repeating the process, leaving success unattained because we never actually complete the project. And in life, the projects never end. When you overcome difficulties in one area and triumph, rest assured the next set of challenges will be waiting. But if you paid attention and learned from your mistakes, you have the ingredients to do better next time.

Thomas Edison's completed work was awarded by the Law of Compensation. That is, somewhere along his difficult journey, he paid the price for all the hardships, temporary defeats, and mishaps. Because he stuck with it, he learned, and things were easier the next time around. Many of us don't stick with things long enough, and we find ourselves trying to accomplish something new every few seconds. It's evident we don't believe that what we are doing will manifest our vision. We pay a price for this type of thinking, and that price is fear, uncertainty, difficulty, and inconsistency in everything we do.

William Shakespeare once said, "All things are ready, if our mind be so." He meant that the moment we stop fearing negative probabilities and instead turn on our faith, the things we want will be available for us. Where our perception lies, therein lies all our opportunities. If we can't perceive something happening for us, we miss out on all the opportunities that would allow us to follow our dreams. Mr. Edison believed that although he may have failed a few times, the ingredients needed to turn fear into faith are as follows:

- ✓ Choose to succeed, and believe that you can.
- ✓ Be willing to pay any price to meet your goals.
- ✓ Focus all your energy on going after the thing you really want, regardless of the challenges and difficulties.

Shakespeare's "All is ready, if the mind be so" quote is similar to the phrase "When the student is ready, the teacher will appear." What's interesting about these quotes is the teacher has always been there; it was the student who needed to be ready for the teacher. When we create a clear picture of the life we want, our suffering lessens and our struggles seem easier. With this clear picture in mind, we are finally ready to be taught by life, and no longer give our energy and power to situations that do not serve us moving forward. Instead, we give our energy and power to our God-like abilities. Where our attention goes, the energy flows. When we take our attention away from fear by believing in our dreams and our ability to accomplish them, our fear turns into faith.

Faith and fear cannot occupy our minds at the same time. One or the other will dominate, so decide today that you will allow faith to dominate you. You can do that by creating positive things to have faith in. If you don't know where to start, here are some ideas:

What do you want your life to look like? This is one of the most important questions to ask yourself, because it makes you finally take ownership of your ability to create the future of your dreams. *You* finally decide: "This is what I want my life to look like" and make it happen, instead of waiting until situations appear and then saying, "No, I don't want my life to look like this."

Who do you want to be? We can be anybody we want to be, but we often fail to be our best selves. Take charge of your life by creating a new image—the person you desire to be—and do what you must each day to make that image true.

What do you want to accomplish? Is it the business you always wanted to start? Get a new job? Write your book? Begin helping the less fortunate? Finding the person you dreamed of marrying? Do you want to be a certain weight? Finish school? Buy a home? Save money? Take a trip around the world? Begin again after a setback? You must have an organized list of the things you want to accomplish to ensure you are on the right path to reaching them.

Take a moment to answer the questions below. This should help you determine which obstacles have caused you to sit on the sidelines of life in fear. Decide today to turn your fear into faith.

1.   Think about a moment when you did not decide to do something. Do you live in regret because of it?

2.   What are three things stopping you from moving forward? Is there anything you can do to change at least one of those things? Why or why not?

3.   Are you currently running away from difficult circumstances? Why? If you were to face them, how

would your life be better? List three steps you can take immediately to change your situation.

4. What has stopped you from jumping into the rope of happiness? Think of the main difficulty holding you back, and draw a circle in the center of a piece of paper. In the circle, write the root cause of your obstacle. Around the main circle, draw several smaller circles filled with solutions or possibilities. Draw a line that links each circle back to the main circle. Get active. Consider each solution or possibility until one of them goads you ahead.

5. List five things you can do today that can turn your fear into faith.

CHAPTER 5

Release Your Doubts and Drop the Burdens

Tis easy enough to be pleasant, when
life flows along like a song; but the man
worthwhile is the one who will smile
when everything goes dead wrong.
—Ella Wheeler Wilcox

The Commitment

Right now, you may be facing one of the most challenging times in your life. The world may be upside down, and everything seems to be a dead end. But what if I told you that you could have everything you've ever desired? All the dreams, all the wishes can be fulfilled, but you must commit to leaving those challenging times behind.

Here is the true challenge: to get the things we desire, we have to leave behind the things we *don't* desire. We cannot commit to being in two places at the same time. Know that taking that first step requires us to commit to *not* going back.

I was watching the movie *Groundhog Day* recently, and the main character, Phil Conners, runs into an old high school friend, Ned "Needle Nose" Ryerson. Ned was a dork in high school who became a life insurance agent. Ned explains who he was and what he did back then, but Phil is not interested and begins walking away. Doing his best to catch up, Ned tries to sell him insurance. As Phil is still walking away, Ned jumps in front of him and asks what he is doing later and if they can get dinner. Phil declines the offer and desperately tries to put some distance between himself and annoying Ned. He steps off the curb and into a puddle of slush almost as high as his knee.

Ned then laughs and says, "Watch out for that first step. It's a doozy."

The look on Phil's face is pure disgust. He knows he can't stay there dealing with the leg full of slush or Ned's constant talking. So he does the only thing he can—he pulls his leg out of the icy water and gets out of there, heading towards where he'd rather be.

Often, this is where we find ourselves when taking the first step toward our dream. Usually, we are forced into taking it, and it's tough and unfamiliar. Because we can't see what's next, it may take all our energy and courage to commit to it. But this is our chance to leave behind the known that we don't want, and head into the unknown that we do want. Even if the first step is a doozy, and people laugh at the initial plunge, just know that what you believe in that moment *after* you take the step will determine if you step forward into growth or run back to safety.

The first step to commitment is a doozy. It's the step away from where we are to where we actually want to go. The first step is the toughest, because it's not far from the place we are most familiar. That means it's easy to go back and go back fast. In the past, we may have been inspired to live a great life. Maybe we were even committed to building one. But a few hours, days, months, or years later, we find ourselves going in the same direction we previously wanted out of. Why? Because we never held ourselves accountable for the current state of our lives. We didn't realize a new life requires major changes, which means serious commitment. If we are honest with ourselves, we realize that we do commit to certain things, but only when it aligns with our perceived reality, and then we live in fear.

A life filled with fear of the future destroys our chances of taking action. If we focus too much on hurt, upset, hardships and setbacks, we commit to those fears. We then spend our time committed to how hard life is. Life never seems to get any easier, and the struggle never goes away. We wake up expecting adversity, and adversity has a way of not disappointing.

We are by nature susceptible to all negative suggestions— things we say to ourselves in those dark moments, those alone times when the world seems to press heavily on our shoulders and the trials of life do not seem to make sense. Or we allow the doubt spoken by others to rule our brain, and we believe their words confirm that we can't live the life of our dreams. We let our circumstances outweigh what we really want by believing that this may be all there is to life. In reality, there is so much more to life for us, but what we choose to do in these most difficult times determines whether we discover all that life has to offer.

Even though something deep down inside may be telling us, "It's too hard. I'll never get the life I want," don't give up. Don't listen to that voice, and don't commit to it. That voice comes from self-imposed limitations running wild right before we finally get up and go after our dream. Instead, get started right away. Immediately after we are inspired, we must commit to taking action, and then *take* action.

Ralph Waldo Emerson once said, "What we fear of doing most is usually what we most need to do." We've remained seated on the sidelines long enough, watching, waiting, hoping things will change. But the people who get to live the life of their dreams look at how they want life to be and commit to the journey, regardless of their current circumstances. They believe that if they have an image of something better, something greater, that image will pull them through the journey.

The moment we make a commitment, we no longer have to worry about what's going wrong; what's going wrong no longer matters. It's making things right that is important.

A well-defined place in my life is where I must get to. It's the place of my hopes, happiness, and dreams fulfilled. I'm willing to give everything I am in exchange for that life.

When we made past commitments and did not stay with them, often, there were no obvious consequences. However, committing is much harder to do when your life has been full of years of broken commitments. Commitments challenge you to be what you said you would be and do what you said you would do, which ultimately allows you to have what you said you would have. Commitment causes us to say, "You know what, life isn't what I want it to be now, but it will be what I want in the future." So if you are stuck and it seems as if you have become a magnet to life's hard knocks, here are some ways to attract success, instead.

- ✓ Decide that by any means, you will win.
- ✓ Focus on where you want to be.
- ✓ Commit yourself to developing the determination to get you there.

Commit to the idea that whatever you are going through is not going to last forever. The life you want to live is larger than where you are, and it's going to require more from you to get there. You'll be required to become a magnet to your ideas, goals, and dreams. Becoming a magnet means you'll attract success by developing a goal-oriented life and growing into a better version of yourself (mentally, physically, and spiritually).

Ask yourself: "Am I attracting my dream, or am I repelling it by staying where I am?"

Marcus Aurelius, the great Roman Emperor, once said, "A man's life is what he makes of it." So it's safe to say if we fail to make a plan for the good we desire in life, we can plan to fail at achieving it. If there is no plan for our future, it will be designed by someone else—and I'm sure if we truly decided to design our life knowing the unlimited possibilities we possess, we would do a much better job than anyone else.

Are You the One?

There is a fictional story from the mid-1700s about Sinbad the Sailor. Sinbad had many voyages at sea, but the one with the Old Man of the Sea stuck out to me the most. The Old Man of the Sea was a trickster who lured travelers into letting him ride on their shoulders while transporting him across the streams. While traveling, the Old Man would not release his grip on the poor person he was riding, forcing him wherever he pleased and allowing his victims little rest. The Old Man's victims all eventually died from this horrible treatment, never making it where they set out to go.

Sinbad was tricked as well. The Old Man hung on to him, taking the life out of him until he almost suffered the same fate as the other travelers. However, Sinbad, even in his weakness, decided his fate would not be determined by another. He would find a way to escape because his destiny meant more to him than any obstacles. He changed his ideas about how to reach his goal, but he never lost sight of it. After getting the Old Man drunk with wine, Sinbad was able to shake him off and kill him.

Most of us have dealt with an "Old Man" in our lives that clings to us and is difficult to shake off. We let him stay there and ride us away from the life we want, allowing the Old Man to take our energy. When we realize we are not going in the direction of our dreams, we try to get rid of him. But by then, most of our energy has been drained from carrying his weight and trying to fight him off. And while we may not die physically, we die mentally.

Like the travelers, we become victims of challenges. Too often, it's almost as if we enjoy the victim role, as if we secretly take pride in this "woe is me" type of thinking. The moment we remove our victim mentality, we feel lost. Sinbad realized that while he was a victim of the trickery of the Old Man, he did not have to remain so. We must realize, as Sinbad did, that the power to overcome the weight life puts upon our shoulders is within ourselves. We must stop looking for outside help and using negative experiences as the reasons we can't live. Only then will we be able to tap into our own infinite resources and discover that we are the ones who can get us to the destination of our choosing.

Often in life, we become distracted by the things we don't want. In doing so, many people go to the grave with a life unfilled and their desires unmet because they never moved toward where they truly wanted to go. Maybe it was just too much to change at the time, or they were too young, too old, too busy with life, too tired, or had no money. Whatever it was, they went their entire lives using that same story.

Building the life of your dreams will mean you are busy, but busy building the life you want. Ask yourself right now, what do you really expect in your life at the present time? Be very honest with yourself. It may be shocking to learn that the Old Man of the Sea that tried to bring Sinbad down is actually *your* negative ideas, which you let control your thoughts about yourself.

Here is a question I have for you today: Why should you not expect the greatest and best life possible? It's not too late to expect great things, regardless of what you have gone through. Money may be at an all-time low, but that does not mean you can't expect abundance. You may be sick, but expect to be well. If you are unhappy, look at the opportunities you have and find a way to create happiness.

All of life wants you to be healthy, happy, and free. There is nothing outside of you that is demanding you live a life that you don't want.

Blazing a New Trail

Achieving the life of your dreams is going to require you to do things differently. By different, I mean if what you are doing now has not yielded the results you want, you have to go completely in the opposite direction, and at all costs. Wanting more out of life means you must develop a drive for it, a burning desire to have the life of your dreams. When you want something bad enough, there is nothing that will stop you from setting sail on a new journey—the journey of having your wishes fulfilled.

Are you willing to do the things today that others won't do in order to have the things tomorrow that others won't have? That's what a risk-taker is.

American author, businessman, and psychiatrist, David Viscott, once said, "If you cannot risk, you cannot grow. If you cannot grow, you cannot become your best. If you cannot become your best, you cannot be happy." And if you cannot be happy, what else is there? What else is there to life if you're not risking the good for the great? What else is there to life if you cannot grow? What else is there if you cannot become your best? Not trying for your true happiness is the recipe for a life unfulfilled.

When the storms of life come, this is not the time to turn off your engines and coast along. It's time to chart a new path by taking a risk. Whenever a ship is in a storm, the captain does not allow the storm to just drift his vessel anywhere. He knows the importance of getting to the destination safely with the people and cargo. He also knows that drifting always leads to danger, and so he takes control of the ship.

For people who don't want to live anymore, that danger is often the "easy way." But for those of us who are determined to win in life, that is the time to turn on the steam and fight against the winds. There is something deep within us that thrives on difficulties, thrives on the risk; it means more than the effort to win. We need to blaze new trails, and in those new trails, we will encounter new hardships that will help us tap into our full potential.

I saw a tree recently that was surrounded by a rock. This was an unusual sight, because the rock actually had a hole in it, which meant the tree had to break through it in order to grow. It knew it wanted to live, so it had to take the risk of trying to get to the life it desired to have at all costs. That tree's growth process was certainly difficult, with each day bringing the chance of failure from lack of sun, broken branches, or even getting washed off the rock in a rainstorm—along with all the same challenges that other trees face.

But this tree didn't say, "I'm going to stay buried beneath this rock and never allow my goals to be achieved or my dreams to materialize." Instead, it said, "I'm going to take a risk. My life is worth living, and whatever stands in my way, I'm going to break through. Because in me living, I'm helping others live as well."

Don't go where the path may lead, but go
where there is no path and blaze a trail.
                                                                —*Emerson*

If you are ready to make the commitment to the life of your dreams, answering these questions will help get you there:

1. Have you made commitments in the past that you did not fulfill? If so, list three reasons why you don't keep your commitments. Meditate on how you can change this.

2. The first step to achieving goals is always a doozy. What conversations did you have with yourself after you took your first step toward your goals?

3. Do you have an "Old Man" weighing you down in life? Do you have more than one? If so, how will you get rid of them?

4. Designing the life you want requires risks. Are you willing to take a risk for your dreams without any guarantee? Explain.

5. When obstacles come, do you drift with the obstacle or steer toward your port of call? Which will benefit you most?

CHAPTER 6

The Challenge is Big, But the Dream Must be Bigger

When one door of happiness closes,
another opens; but often we look so long
at the closed door that we do not see the
one which has been opened for us.
                                        —*Helen Keller*

Are You Prepared for the Storm?

Running is very therapeutic for me. Once I'm outside, no matter what's going on in my life, I seem to find the answers I'm looking for. Not long ago, I challenged myself to get up at 5:00 a.m. and add more miles to my run. So the night before, I promised myself nothing was going to stop me. Ironically, everything that could keep me up the night before, did.

My alarm clock buzzed at 4:50 a.m. I knew what time it was—time to get going. Still lying in bed, my mind started roaming, almost as if it were arguing with me. *Today is not the day for you to run. Why don't you wait until tomorrow? You can get the six-pack you want back in two weeks if you start then.*

I knew the reason for the mental and physical delay was simple: I had planned to run on one of the toughest routes. There is an extremely high bridge along the route, and I imagined every obstacle and challenge; it was all I could think of. Instead of seeing myself complete my goal, my vision was on how hard it would be. *It's so dark outside, no one will be running. There are steep inclines on both sides of the bridge, so either direction is a challenge.*

I stood up to that argument. "No, I have to move now because this is not what I wanted, and I need to get up." But at that time, I started delaying and delaying and delaying. I call that "hitting the snooze button."

After forty-five minutes of tug of war, I rushed out of my house. As I reached the middle of the bridge, I glanced over to look at the sky, and it was filled with a dark-purple color. I thought, *This can't be good,* but I kept running. On my way back over the bridge, I got an alert on my phone about a severe thunderstorm approaching in three minutes. Based on my timeline, it would take me about twenty minutes to get home, so I had no option but to weather this storm. In exactly three minutes the sky opened, and rain came down like I'd never seen before. There were three decisions I had to make:

1. Do I continue running through the storm?
2. Do I step off to the side and wait for it to stop?
3. Do I slow down and just throw my hands up in defeat?

I decided to keep running, and as the rain soaked my clothes, right away I understood the compound effect of me not getting up forty-five minutes earlier.

In life, we are always rushing, always moving, and while a storm can be on the horizon, too often we simply are not prepared. Usually, the consequences of our actions in the past do not cost us right away. If they did, we would make radical adjustments immediately. But instead, we feel as if we can just keep putting off our life and pushing off our dreams, our health, and our family. In the process, we live aimlessly, allowing the storms to keep coming.

If your idea of what you want outweighs what you don't want, then you won't sit around waiting in life. You know the temporary adjustment may be a little uncomfortable at first, but waiting any longer comes with a hefty price to pay. You must zero in on the things you want.

Zeroing In

When a photographer is taking a photo, they adjust the lens of the camera so the picture is captured as they wish to see it. When we focus on something, whether good or bad, we also clearly see the thing we are focusing on. This is the image we carry, and this is what we zero in on. In doing this, we attract whatever it is we clearly see and bring it right into our lives. By giving our goals all our attention, our thoughts become our feelings, which become our actions that allow our goals to manifest. When we know this, we will spend more time zeroing in on and capturing the good that we desire so that our actions reflect our thoughts and our thoughts reflect our actions.

Hellen Keller once said, "When one door closes, another door opens. We spend so much time giving attention to closed doors in our life that we don't see all the open doors."

While the storms of life do come and go, just like the one I faced when running, I finally started paying attention to something. I had always assumed storms got worse before they got better, but did they really? In truth, they don't; that was my own perception. It's what I told myself during the times of adversity. I zeroed in on all the negative things until I paralyzed myself and found storms all around me. Storms don't actually get worse before they get better, they get as bad as we tell ourselves they are. So before we start giving all of our power away to a storm, what lessons can we learn from it to be better prepared next time?

Like me, we all have three choices to make. We can keep going through it, focusing on a positive outcome, we can stop and wait for the storm to pass, or we can just get beat up by the storm. I call that "slowing down." Only when we *believe* we are stronger than the storms of life (when we come to understand our truest wants) will we start to zero in on a better life. At this stage, nothing else matters but our dreams, nothing else matters but our goals, nothing else matters but the life we want to live. As Thomas Jefferson once said, "Nothing can stop the man with the right mental attitude from achieving his goal; nothing on earth can help the man with the wrong mental attitude."

What are the storms in your life that you have been focused on? Is it worrying things won't turn around for you? Health issues? The economy? Family troubles? What have you been giving your time and energy to, not realizing that where your attention goes, your energy flows? Think about all the good that would come into your life if you withdrew the energy you gave to all the things going wrong. Think about what you would be able to accomplish if today you made a choice to think about all the things going right.

What we zero in on with the lens of our mind determines where we ultimately end up. The challenge for many is the difficulty of paying attention until the dream is complete. We want our goals to instantly manifest the moment they pop into our minds, and when we don't see them happen quickly, we don't trust the process. We find ourselves paying attention to too many other things. In most cases, we even feel it's hard to pay attention to one thing, and it's much wiser to do a bunch of things at one time. This is where the term "spreading ourselves thin" comes in: I'm doing too much in too many places at one time.

Please ponder this question: "How can I be productive and accomplish what I truly want without spreading myself thin?"

To achieve the life of our dreams, it's important to know what we want and hold tight to that until it happens. That's giving undivided attention to your dreams. It means shutting out everything else. When we pay attention to the ideas that motivate and dominate our minds daily, it is those that we act upon. It is those that we go after.

How to Zero In

Imagine what you want your life to really look like. Surprisingly, this can be one of the toughest things to do. With the speed of how fast things come at us daily, paying attention to dreams and goals can become challenging. We get distracted, our actions don't always follow our ideas, and life for us becomes a wild tornado. Understand that in order to walk in the direction of the life we want to live, we must know what that life is.

Focus

When we focus, we are centered on one thing rather than multitasking. The thing we want becomes narrow. We direct all our attention to it. It's the *only* thing we concentrate on. Focus requires clarity. You must be clear about what you want so you can see it, zoom in, and go after it.

No Distractions

Our progress in life comes from our increased attention to the things we are trying to achieve. While distractions do come, and they come often, their job is to take us away from where we want to be. Too often, when a distraction comes, we feel we must sit and work with it before we get back to our dreams. Yes, distractions will come, but please know that distractions will always be there, especially if we are looking for them.

Adjust Your Lens

At first, it may be hard to determine exactly what you want your life to look like. You just might not have a clear idea of it. All you know is what you are dealing with now is not what you want. It is important to start spending time with your goals, writing things down, thinking about them, and planning things out. In this way, you can adjust your lens so you can see clearer.

Clarify Your Dreams

It's been said, "Wherever you find yourself in life, at some point in time, you made an appointment to be there." If you are not currently where you want to be, this can be a tough pill to swallow. But it's time to own up to it and face it. It's time to get real with YOURSELF. Don't stay in what you know is not right for your life because you never got clarity on what you wanted your life to look like.

Perhaps you had goals or dreams that you wanted to accomplish, but you didn't want to go through the storms for them. You didn't want to try. People who stay in this mental space are called "volunteer victims." They complain about their position in life, the circumstances they face, where they work, what's going on with the world, and why they can't get ahead. They live in fear. They allow everything to happen to them.

Here is the truth: nobody is making them live like that. Things have happened in all our lives that did not work out the way we expected. That does not mean we should give up our dreams. Don't allow fear or embarrassment to discourage you from getting up and doing what you want to do. Don't beat yourself up; you've beaten yourself up long enough. People have beaten you down long enough. You've listened to the negative conversation, and it brought you here. Don't listen to that negative voice again. Get clear on your thinking and carve out a new life for yourself. Go back to those dreams you wanted. If they are not as strong as they used to be, perhaps they're not something you want anymore. What do you want now?

Contrary to popular belief, just because you did not accomplish those goals from the past does not mean you are a failure. You do not have to live with that for the rest of your life. *You* can decide to change it. Remember, to excel in the next grade in life, we have to learn all that is necessary in the grade we are at the moment. There's nothing to be embarrassed about, except wasting another day living a life that is not you. It may be a job, a business, a relationship, or a decision that you made. Make a change! Life and time are too precious to continue living a lie. You deserve better, and you can do better when you get the courage to do what you know you must: live the life you desire.

Is the life you want to live worth it? You have to believe that it is. No matter where you are right now, you can make the decision today to adjust your dreams.

> *A man may imagine things that are false,*
> *but he can only understand things that*
> *are true, for if the things be false, the*
> *apprehension of them is not understanding.*
> —*Sir Isaac Newton*

There has never been a better time to Wake Up and Live the life of your dreams. Answer the questions below to give yourself a boost in that direction.

1. Have you found yourself in the storms of life, believing that life is one big, repeated storm? If yes, knowing that we give our storms power, how will you handle your perceived storms going forward?

2. What have you put off doing for years that you are paying the consequences for today? Knowing these consequences, what immediate changes can you make now?

3. Do you spend more time zeroing in on negative things in life but wishing for a positive outcome? If yes, how has this affected your ability to receive the good in life?

4. When doors close in your life, how much time do you spend trying to open them rather than looking for other open doors? Explain.

5. Have you become a volunteer victim? If so, what three things can you do today to adjust your dream?

CHAPTER 7

Your Future Begins with You

The whole secret of a successful life is to find
out what is one's destiny to do,
and then do it.

—*Henry Ford*

Bigger than You

R ecently, my sons brought home some dirt in a small
container. They planted a seed in the dirt from a pack
of seeds, filled with so much excitement about what
would one day spring forth out of this small amount of dirt.
Every day they made sure they watered the seed and provided
it with sunlight. After a few weeks of consistency, we finally
saw small green life emerge from the dirt. Reminiscing on my
time in school, I found myself thinking how powerful it is that
this tiny seed always has life, but when it was wrapped up in

the package, it was not living. The moment it's put in the soil, however, it becomes active and gathers all the necessary elements around it to grow into its full potential.

The plant has one job: grow to its fullest potential so it can produce thousands of seeds, which will, in turn, grow to produce more seeds. It is its natural life cycle to continue advancing toward more life; life is always seeking expression. Our purpose is the same way—it's constantly seeking expression through us. All our untapped, limitless potential is trapped inside of us, begging to get out. Begging to show our greatness, begging to be used, begging to leave a mark on this earth while we are here.

When I ask people about some of the things they want to accomplish in life, I'm usually met with: "I want to accomplish this or that, but . . ." Below is a list of common excuses people give for not completing their goals:

- too old
- too young
- things happened that set me back years ago
- growing up was hard
- no money now
- I need to wait until I get things in order
- bad marriage
- didn't finish school
- homeless
- incarcerated

And the list goes on. If you also fall to these excuses, then you have accepted a negative idea about who you are and how valuable you are to the world. But let me tell you why you really didn't achieve the dream. You have not yet realized there is something inside of you that is much larger than yourself. Like the seed trapped in a package, you have a full life awaiting expression. And if you are not expressing yourself, you are not living. You need a bigger dream, and just as the seed's one function is to grow to its fullest potential, you also must grow into your fullest potential. Not just grow and do nothing thereafter, but continue to express your life by living it well.

If you are stuck, then your dream is not large enough. It doesn't inspire, it doesn't cause you to reach and expand, and you have not envisioned what life would be once you become what you want to be. You've thought about it, perhaps even daydreamed. Still, you were not strong enough to gather all the necessary elements around you to grow into your full potential. If you are at this point in life, I have news for you: You don't have to stay here, and your dreams can still be accomplished.

In speaking with a client recently, we talked about a New Year's Resolution. He promised this would be the year he would finally accomplish his goals. I asked him what he thought had been his challenge before. He said, "Every year, I just roll over my goals from the year before."

I laughed as I was reminded of a cell phone company that used to have rollover minutes. The minutes we didn't use in the months prior rolled over to the next month. Unfortunately, we also do that with our goals and dreams. We just roll them over year after year. As a result, they start to become stale and uninspiring; they are no longer strong enough to pull us through the difficult times. What we may be facing does not outweigh what we want. So my response was, "Perhaps we have to go back to the drawing board and create some new goals and commit to larger dreams."

Dreams should be like a magnet, they pull you through the tough times, those hard times—those dark moments when all seems lost and there is no one to turn to. It's in those moments that we think about what's bigger than ourselves. If you are constantly weighed down by all the things going wrong, how can you grow? A plant in a bad environment will wither away. So does the mind that's in a negative mental environment. If you are not growing, how can you possibly focus on making an impact? How can you possibly focus on the lives you want to change? The business you want to open? The books you want to write or the world you want to travel? How can you focus on the legacy you want to leave for your family, or on the people you have not met yet whose lives you will change?

This is the purpose of more life for you; this is why you must grow to your fullest potential. You can't do any of these things if you are constantly down and out, worrying, fearing tomorrow, or running away from adversity. You have to see your future and ask yourself, "Who am I?" and "Why am I here?" We all have a purpose to fulfill in life.

Consider these questions:

1. What do you really want?
2. Who do you really want to be?
3. What do you really want to accomplish?

Answering these questions for yourself gives your life meaning and hope. Hope for the future gives you the power in the present. You see what this new future looks like, and you imagine it day in and day out.

Albert Einstein once said, "Imagination is everything. It is the preview of life's coming attractions." Know how powerful you are, and that life is about living—and living to your fullest potential gives you more life in the process.

Time to Get Moving

The biggest challenge in all our lives is internal: How do I begin to find my purpose? Most of us have an idea of what we want to do. But often, it's something we saw or someone told us was right for us. We did not choose it for ourselves, and we are not so sure if it's right. This causes an inner conflict. For many years, we struggle with who we want to be and what we want. We can't seem to make the choice and just do something. We become idle, and we don't begin anything.

When we don't take action, we will find our thoughts stagnated—the two go together. We might let other people decide what we want to be. But life is big, with limitless possibilities, and the key is to realize we can accomplish anything we desire when we understand this.

Sometimes, we look to the external to judge our internal progress. We may spend too much time seeing how other people are doing, even if they are not successful at it. Comparing your life with someone else's always causes an inner conflict.

Think about a lily for a moment. They work in silence and grow so beautifully, but the work is done as an *inside* process; they don't focus on the progress of other lilies. Too many times, we are focused on the external, trying to work out our problems by making sure we have the material things we seek. But in this distracted hurry, we forget about the work that is required to grow. Like the lilies of the field, we must be patient and grow into our best expressions of ourselves. We should always remember that the things we want are external ideas, but to obtain them, we have to grow—and that is an internal process.

As the plant grows, it requires more nutrients, sun and soil. If it's not getting what it needs, it will eventually wither away and die. Like the plant, we need our own nutrients if we are going to discover, grow, and develop into our fullest. While we may not know exactly what we want right away, it's important to get moving toward something. You need to find your purpose—and it's not going to come to you on its own.

Make it a point to decide today what you want to accomplish. Be sure the choice you make will be the most satisfactory, the one that gives your life full meaning. Consider what truly makes you happy.

Remember, choosing your life's purpose is an internal process. Other people cannot decide what is best for you. Although it is important to consider the wisdom of others, only you can truly decide what you want to be. Too often, we waste time trying to get advice from people who are not in our position or have never accomplished what we are trying to accomplish, and this is usually why we never get moving.

While people may often offer well-meaning advice, we have also all been subjected to the negative thoughts of others. It's subtle, and it usually comes from the people we are close to. Be sure to safeguard what you want to do, keep your conversations limited, and let your actions show that you are determined to get the thing you want to accomplish.

> *Great things are done by people who think*
> *great thoughts, and then go out into the*
> *world to make their dreams come true.*
> —Ernest Holmes

Hold Your Dream to a High Standard

A man bought several acres of land to build a new home. On the weekends, he drove out to his property to work on the grounds for his new building. All the rocks were replaced with trees and flowers. The work was challenging and tiring, but thinking of his finished new home lightened the hard work needed to get to the dream.

One day, a real estate agent drove up to the property with a disturbing look on his face. The agent asked the man whether he had been hired to improve the property.

"No," the owner responded. "I'm the owner of this land."

The agent walked to his car and came back with some paperwork, which proved the man was not the owner of the property. A mistake in paperwork revealed he actually owned the acres *next* to this particular property. So all that time, he had been working hard on something that was not his.

The man confirmed the information and accepted the mistake. He moved over to the other piece of land and once again set to work, making it all he desired. He was determined to make his dream come true, despite the setback.

No one ever fully sees the steps they must take in reaching a certain end. They may see a general way they must proceed from one point to another, but all the details are not definite unless they have gone through this before. Like the man working on the wrong property, we must be able to look at where we are

69

in life. If we find that we have been working on the wrong plan to get to the dream, we change the plan—but not the dream.

In life, there will be times when we are required to acknowledge our errors. Admitting that we have done nothing for ourselves over the years but build something for someone else can be shocking. When we finally do, however, we can begin to work for ourselves.

Napoleon Bonaparte, the great war general, was once a half-starved lieutenant. Still, he always saw himself as the general of armies and the master of France. Like Napoleon, we must see ourselves as the greatest possible version of ourselves, regardless of where we are now in life.

This can be extremely difficult, because our outward lives do not mirror what we envisioned right away. We must see ourselves doing and having all that we set out to do, even when we start from nothing. We may not recognize the moment of our change, because that change started the moment we decided to make it so. But as time goes by, we will find that our ideas are broader and our limited worldview has been transformed. We will find our mind more alert, and we will see clearly, whereas we were in doubt before.

We have begun thinking about unlimited possibilities, instead of appearances.

We must understand that the moment we decide on our goal is not the moment we become what we want, but it *is* the moment we act. The action starts the process of moving toward the goal. This, I realize, is why starting has been so challenging all along. Usually, at this point, we hurry; we want things to happen on our own time, or the moment we finally see the beauty in our lives. We finally get that glimpse. And it is amazing.

Like anything that's considered beautiful in its completed state, often we don't see the growth process it took to get to that state. This is why the vision for the dream is so important. Growing can be difficult, especially when you don't know you have to grow. The adjustments can be painful, the setbacks can hurt. Yes, we may have financial issues, family issues, or career and school issues that are pressing for a fast solution. Yes, those things have to be done, but if we don't have the trust and the confidence that our goals will be, we will continue building on the wrong property. Knowing what you are working for and what will one day soon appear is the reason you must hold your dream to a high standard.

1.   I want you to think about your goals and dreams today. If you have not accomplished your goals, you may be rolling over uninspiring goals. Write down five goals you have not accomplished in the last two years.

2.   What are three reasons you feel you have not accomplished these five goals?

3. With this same list, do you feel the same today as you did when you initially determined what you wanted to accomplish, or are you rolling over your goals?

4. If these goals are still inspiring to you, what can you do differently today that will help you take a small step in the direction of those goals?

5. Is it easy for you to admit that change is inevitable? Why or why not?

CHAPTER 8

Life is Not Over, Get Back in The Race

Nothing happens by chance,
everything is pushed from behind
—Ralph Waldo Emerson

The Will to Live

In life, when things are not turning out the way we think they should, the first thing we do is become impatient and upset. Even though we tell ourselves that life is full of ups and downs, we still react badly in the moment. If we know that life brings uncertainty, then why are we so ill-equipped to handle those down times? When things don't turn out the way we think they should, why do we freak out?

When we panic and become impatient, we are saying: "I don't trust the journey to my dreams. I want what I want, and it has to happen now."

We must remember that while the journey to our dreams may send us on a wild detour, we still have power over ourselves and what we do. How we apply ourselves during the difficult and unexpected times will determine if we reach our goals.

Oftentimes, we judge life according to appearances. We prefer routine and safety, so once calamity thunders down upon us, we assume the end of our life is near, no matter how much living we have left. We may experience something traumatic, something difficult, and feel we just don't possess the energy to try anymore. We are tapped out and left feeling hopeless, powerless. We may know everything we need to do, but we are emotionally drained.

Instead of looking for the answers and strength inside, we find ourselves looking for something external to take us away from this place to a paradise that we can't even describe—as long as it's better than where we are. Life's obstacles have wiped us out, and we don't even recognize ourselves anymore.

People ask, "What's wrong with them? They used to have it all. So confident and energetic, such a will to live."

If we are honest with ourselves, unexpected events happen that seem to just zap the life out of us. Sometimes, we may lose it when our daily lives are turned upside down. When this happens, we have to remember that we don't have to always have everything together, and life won't be perfect. What is necessary is that we develop the will to live, the will to win—that we stand up to life and dig in. There is an incredible life waiting for you, but you must first become aware of its existence. You can obtain your best life by specifically designing it.

Give Life a Chance

Every morning when we wake up, it's important to start the day ready to live our best life, no matter what life may throw our way. Stand up, take a deep breath and say, "Okay, life, I'm ready. I'm ready to win, I'm ready to live." Deep down, we must know exactly what we are striving for and working toward. We have to believe that at the end of it all, "I am going to win!"

Life right now may not be the way we planned. There will be some hard decisions, some uncertainty. We may be overwhelmed, but we must realize that this is a painful part of the process called life. Too much of the time, we only see the negative. We only see the bad things happening, and we wonder why good things don't come our way. The truth is, good things come our way too, but we are unable to recognize them because we are not paying attention.

The British historian and essayist Thomas Carlyle once said, "Most people without a purpose can be compared to a ship without a rudder." In other words, they live in neutral. If the wind blows one way, they go in that direction. If the wind blows another way, they go that way. They don't have a real destination, so they don't have any direction. Therefore, they never get where they wanted.

You must determine where you will end up! You have to say, "You know what, life, there is more to this, and I'm willing to get what's mine." Yes, there may be some challenges and dark moments. There may be some roads that are tougher than we thought. Some roads we may have asked to travel and others we did not—but if we are on the path to our goals, they are the roads we must travel.

When we asked for a better life filled with happiness, joy, love, and the dream, what price did we think we would pay? When we did not choose what we wanted, did we think we were avoiding paying a price? The fact is, there is a price to pay no matter what choices we make—so why not pay the price for the life you desire?

Now is not the time to quit. If you have been living below your expectations for life, decide today you are no longer going to live this way. Instead, see your goals accomplished, and see yourself living and winning. Don't wait for tomorrow or for things to change. Start now wherever you are, with whatever you have.

Life is about experience, and these experiences will change us during our journey. During the trying times, we must ask ourselves: "Who am I becoming because of this?"

When skyscrapers are built, they must dig deep in the ground, almost twice the size of the building's actual height. Why? Because the foundation must be strong to keep the building from falling, and the only way to do that is by digging deep. When you discover the will to live, you discover a part of you that you just did not know was there. You no longer dig on the surface, because you realize the surface things are shallow. It may look nice on the outside, but there is no depth to it.

It's time to stop digging on the surface levels of life and start digging deep down into the bedrock. Too many years have gone by, and we have been building life on quicksand. This is why things have been falling apart during every storm. Quicksand can't hold anything. It's time to start going down to the bedrock of your soul and building foundations there. It's time to build your dreams and goals on a solid foundation so that this time, they manifest.

Life was not designed to be this endless circle of pain, guilt, and hurt from the past. Regardless of where you are or what you have experienced, you have to give life a chance. You have to dig deep and find the will to live. This may be difficult to do at the beginning, because we are so focused on all the bad things, the hard times, what went wrong and how things never seem to go right. These things cause us to remain in fear of living a great life—we don't want to lose, and we don't want to fail.

Yet most people fail in life not because they aim high and miss. They fail because they aim low, and that's what they hit. They don't set high standards. They are not willing to go through what's required to live their best, so they go after the things they know they can accomplish, the things that are convenient and comfortable.

Get Back in the Race

I watched an old Olympic race recently, which caused me to think about Murphy's Law. Murphy's Law states: "If anything can go wrong, it will and at the worst possible time." The runner who was supposed to win the race was the favorite. The only thing that would stop him was the unthinkable. Guess what happened—the unthinkable. As the runners are running, he gets tripped by another runner, and he stumbles. Other runners are stepping over him or on him, even on his head. This is the Olympics; this is what he has trained so hard for. How can this possibly happen? As all the people in the stadium were gasping at this event in complete shock (myself included), I said, "Listen, man, stay down. Sit this one out. That was a nasty fall. It's over."

In life, when there are setbacks, people will see the adversity and say, "We feel sorry for you, and we know the trouble you may be facing. Why don't you give yourself some time off? Sit this one out, you don't need to get back in the race."

But this runner had worked hard to get to this stage in life. He'd already faced enough challenges just being there. He got back up, and with only a split second, he had to make a decision: *Do I want to win this race?*

So he got back in the race and started to run again. Soon, he caught up to the pack ahead of him, and then kept running past them—finally passing the leaders. Not only did he get back in the race, but he won the race. The Olympian gave himself a chance to win because he didn't quit when he met with temporary defeat.

Stumbling could have provided him with the ammunition to say, "This race is over. Everyone saw what happened to me. They cheated, and I will use this as my excuse." But here is what was so powerful about the runner: he never focused on the adversity or the other runners. The only thing he focused on was winning the race.

Often in life, we are not focused on anything specific, so we are running after unfulfilling ideas, casual goals, and expired dreams that are no longer inspiring. We are not really running after our purpose, not really running after the dream or the goal. Therefore, when the challenge comes or Murphy's Law appears, we stay on the sidelines of life, cheering others on, but we won't cheer ourselves on.

Like this Olympic runner, you have to know your true identity. You have to know that there is greater for you. Although he suffered a setback on the biggest stage, he knew to get back in the race and try again. He knew that if he did not, he would not be true to his goal. He could not quit and disqualify himself. So, he got back in the race and gave it all he had.

The crowd watching him didn't see what he saw inside himself. They may have looked at him and said, "Too bad," or asked, "Oh, is he okay?" But he saw himself winning; the victory was in his mind. He kept saying, "I'm going to turn this thing around and win!"

Whatever your goals are in life, go after them with everything you've got. Not one foot in and one foot out. Things will happen and you may get knocked down. You may have to get back up gingerly and slowly to start your race again, but the important thing is that you get back in the race.

You can't get upset when things don't work out. Strong people have strong purposes, and strong purposes lead to great achievements. You must know who you truly are. You must believe that just because things are going left in life does not mean you go left with them. It does not matter what happened before. What does matter is what you want to happen now.

Even if the whole world is looking at you, even if they all saw you fall—get up and get back in the race.

You Can Fly

When an eagle has baby eagles, they usually nest for about twelve weeks. Eventually, the mother senses when the babies should start to learn to fly. When the time seems right, she takes the baby eagle up out of the nest, brings it to the open sky, and drops it. If the eaglet does not fly, she swoops down to get it and brings it back to its nest safely.

In a few days, she does the same process again, but lets the eaglet fall lower than the previous time. If the baby eagle is still struggling, she swoops in and takes it back to its nest. She repeats the process. Usually on the third time, the baby eagle realizes their wings are strong enough for them to fly, and they no longer need to be tested. They then take off and fly.

Like the eagles, life is asking more of you, and in some cases pushing you to get what you're asking for. If you want to soar to your dreams, you can't expect it to happen sitting in the nest. If you want things to be different in life, you must begin to do things differently. Doing things differently means you are thinking differently—you're thinking positively. Your outlook on life is as a winner, and you know you can fly.

Sometimes we don't realize that life is testing us to see if we are ready to get to the next level, and so we will keep getting tested until we step out and fly. And when we do find our wings, we find we have more control over our life. It is now something worth living, something we can confidently strive for, regardless of whatever is going on in the world.

You must speak confidently and know: *I have greatness in me, so my walk is different. I smile differently, and my conversation is different. I no longer have to tell people I am different; my actions show it.*

Maybe the last time you told the world you were different, and things were going to change, people didn't believe in you. When adversity hit, you were embarrassed, and they laughed at your downfall. This time, you don't have to go out and make an announcement that things will be different. You don't have to prove to anyone you have changed. No one has to see the world drop you before you wake up and live, before you extend your wings and fly. There is something in you that is greater than what you have gone through, or are going through. You have to know that you can live, that you are qualified and that you can win.

If you are having trouble finding your will to live, you will have to dig deep and search. Answering the questions below can help you Wake Up and Live.

1. When you are met with adversity, do you quit, stick things out with no plan, or know this will eventually pass? Explain your answer.

2. Have you found yourself building your dreams and goals on quicksand? If yes, what steps will you take to ensure you are building on a solid foundation?

3. Practice does not mean perfect. It means prepared. Have you put the time in to be prepared for the life you want to live? Please explain and be as detailed as possible.

4. What do you believe about yourself when no one else does?

5. Looking over your experiences in life, like the baby eagle, we may have to be dropped in life a few times before we know we can fly. How have you prepared to fly?

CPSIA information can be obtained
at www.ICGtesting.com
Printed in the USA
LVHW040440210820
663573LV00004B/228